RICO SANCHEZ, DISC JOCKEY

An Automated Business Simulation

This simulation covers the transactions completed by Rico Sanchez, Disc Jockey, a service business organized as a proprietorship. Rico Sanchez, the owner, began his disc jockey business on September 1 of the current year. Rico performs at clubs and private parties. He also specializes in karaoke, upon request. Rico has made arrangements with the owners of two large clubs to allow them to pay for services on the 1st and 15th days of the month. All other customers must pay when the disc jockey (DJ) services are performed.

ACCOUNTING CYCLE

Rico Sanchez, Disc Jockey, uses a one-month fiscal period. The fiscal period for this simulation begins on September 1 and ends on September 30 of the current year.

To complete the automated accounting activities for Rico Sanchez for the period September 1-30 of the current year, you will need the following:

1. *Automated Accounting*
2. The appropriate data file for *Century 21 Accounting*, Ninth Edition, to be used with *Automated Accounting*

The instructions in this booklet assume that you have already become familiar with the *Automated Accounting* software.

Rico Sanchez, Disc Jockey, an Automated Business Simulation is designed to be used with the *Automated Accounting* software. You will use the computer to key and process business transactions, following the step-by-step instructions that lead you through the procedures required to complete this simulation. You may find the appropriate *Automated Accounting* textbook helpful if you want to know more about what the computer is doing or if you need additional operating assistance.

AUDIT REPORTS

Four audit reports are included at the back of this booklet. Information from computer-generated reports is to be recorded on each audit report. You will be instructed when to fill out the audit reports. If you have a printer available with your computer, your instructor may require you to print all reports generated during this simulation. However, if you do not have a printer available, your instructor may require you to display each report on the monitor instead. In this case, each time you display a report, you should check the audit report to see if any information needs to be recorded.

PROBLEM INSTRUCTIONS

Specially-designed step-by-step software operating instructions are available to help you complete this simulation. The instructions are built into the data file. Once your data file is loaded and saved, click the Browser button on your toolbar. The problem instructions will be displayed in your computer's default Internet browser. (You do not need to be online to display these instructions.) These problem instructions are used throughout the simulation.

For ease of reference as you complete the simulation, you may wish to minimize the browser. Then, as you are ready to complete each new step, you can quickly restore the instructions by clicking on the browser name at the bottom of your screen without needing to reload the browser and instructions.

SEPTEMBER 1-14

Throughout this simulation, you will need to refer to the chart of accounts for Rico Sanchez to obtain the account numbers for completing the transactions. The chart of accounts can be displayed or printed by the *Automated Accounting* software.

Step 1 Bring up the *Automated Accounting* system.

Step 2 Select data file SANCHEZ from the appropriate directory/folder.

Step 3 Select File from the menu bar and choose the Save As menu command. Key the path to the drive and directory that contains your data files. Save the data file with a file name of SANCHEZ XXX XXX (where the Xs are your first and last names.

Step 4 Refer to the Problem Instructions.

Step 5 Key the transactions dated September 1-14.

Hand in the audit report for September 1-14 and any printouts to your instructor.

September 1

No. 1. Received cash from the owner, Rico Sanchez, $2,500.00. R1.

September 2

No. 2. Paid monthly rental fee on turntables and other equipment, $680.00. C1. (The business records all rentals in the Rental Expense account when the payment is made.)

No. 3. Paid cash for new music, $350.00. C2. (At the time of purchase, the business records the purchase costs of all music and equipment in the Supplies—Music & Equipment account.)

September 3

No. 4. Paid cash for business insurance, $300.00. C3. (The business records all insurance costs in the Prepaid Insurance account when the payment is made.)

No. 5. Paid cash to establish a petty cash fund, $150.00. C4.

September 4

No. 6. Bought office supplies on account from Office&Home, Inc., $50.00. M1. (The business records the cost of all office supplies in the Supplies—Office account at the time of purchase.)

No. 7. Paid cash for van rental for the month, $275.00. C5.

September 5

No. 8. Paid cash for office rental for the month, $235.00. C6.

September 6

No. 9. Sold DJ service on account to JJ's Dance Club, $500.00. S1.

September 7

No. 10. Sold DJ service for a private party and received cash, $325.00. R2.

September 8

No. 11. Paid cash for advertising in the local paper, $110.00. C7.

No. 12. Sold DJ service for a private party and received cash, $450.00. R3.

September 9

No. 13. Paid cash on account to Office&Home, Inc., $50.00. C8.

No. 14. Paid cash to owner for personal use, $200.00. C9.

September 10

No. 15. Sold DJ service for the high school Fall mixer; received $275.00. R4.

September 11

No. 16. Paid cash for miscellaneous expense, $48.00. C10.

No. 17. Paid cash for repair of equipment, $92.00. C11.

September 12

No. 18. Sold DJ service on account to JJ's Dance Club, $500.00. S2.

September 13

No. 19. Bought equipment supplies on account from Electronics Unlimited, $175.00. M2.

No. 20. Sold DJ service on account to Funky Club, $475.00. S3.

September 14

No. 21. Sold DJ service for a private party; received cash, $450.00. R5.

Compare your trial balance with the trial balance shown in Figure 1. Find and correct any errors before proceeding.

Figure 1 Trial Balance, September 14

Rico Sanchez, Disc Jockey
Trial Balance
09/14/--

Acct. Number	Account Title	Debit	Credit
110	Cash	1510.00	
120	Petty Cash	150.00	
130	A.R.--JJ's Dance Club	1000.00	
140	A.R.--Funky Club	475.00	
150	Supplies--Office	50.00	
160	Supplies--Music & Equip	525.00	
170	Prepaid Insurance	300.00	
220	A.P.--Electronics Unlim.		175.00
310	Rico Sanchez, Capital		2500.00
320	Rico Sanchez, Drawing	200.00	
410	Service Sales		2975.00
510	Advertising Expense	110.00	
530	Miscellaneous Expense	48.00	
560	Rental Expense	1190.00	
570	Repair & Cleaning Expense	92.00	
	Totals	5650.00	5650.00

SEPTEMBER 15-25

Step 1 Bring up the *Automated Accounting* system.

Step 2 Select data file SANCHEZ XXX XXX (where the Xs are your first and last name) from the drive and directory/folder that contains your data files.

Step 3 Refer to the Problem Instructions.

Step 4 Key the transactions dated September 15-25.

Hand in the audit report for September 15-25 and any printouts to your instructor.

September 15

No. 22. Paid cash for miscellaneous expense, $45.00. C12.
No. 23. Received payment due from JJ's Dance Club, $1,000.00. R6.
No. 24. Sold DJ service for a private party; received cash, $625.00. R7.
No. 25. Received payment due from Funky Club, $475.00. R8.

September 16

No. 26. Paid cash for miscellaneous expense, $62.00. C13.
No. 27. Paid cash for advertising on radio, $200.00. C14.

No. 28. Bought new music on account from R&B Music, Inc., $95.00. M3.
No. 29. Sold DJ service for a private party; received cash, $450.00. R9.

September 17

No. 30. Paid cash for van cleaning, $70.00. C15.
No. 31. Paid cash for cell phone bill, $75.00. C16.
No. 32. Paid cash for office supplies, $60.00. C17.
No. 33. Sold karaoke service for charity fundraiser; received cash, $290.00. R10.

September 18

No. 34. Paid amount due to Electronics Unlimited, $175.00. C18.
No. 35. Paid cash to owner for personal use, $250.00. C19.
No. 36. Sold all-day DJ service on account to JJ's Dance Club, $850.00. S4.

September 19

No. 37. Paid cash for miscellaneous expense, $85.00. C20.
No. 38. Sold DJ service on account to JJ's Dance Club, $500.00. S5.

September 20

No. 39. Paid amount due to R&B Music, Inc., $95.00. C21.
No. 40. Bought equipment supplies on account from Electronics Unlimited, $67.00. M4.
No. 41. Sold DJ service on account to JJ's Dance Club, $500.00. S6.

September 21

No. 42. Sold DJ services for the Town Hall Fall Festival; received cash, $375.00. R11.

September 22

No. 43. Bought new music on account from R&B Music, Inc., $145.00. M5.
No. 44. Sold DJ services to the local country club; received cash, $400.00. R12.

September 23

No. 45. Paid cash for cleaning of equipment, $80.00. C22.
No. 46. Paid cash to owner for personal use, $220.00. C23.
No. 47. Sold DJ services for local college dance; received cash, $445.00. R13.

September 24

No. 48. Paid bill for electricity for the month, $83.00. C24.
No. 49. Sold DJ service on account to Funky Club, $490.00. S7.

September 25

No. 50. Sold DJ service on account to Funky Club for marathon dance contest, $1,150.00. S8.

Compare your trial balance with the trial balance shown in Figure 2. Find and correct any errors before proceeding.

Figure 2 Trial Balance, September 25

Rico Sanchez, Disc Jockey
Trial Balance
09/25/--

Acct Number	Account Title	Debit	Credit
110	Cash	4070.00	
120	Petty Cash	150.00	
130	A.R.--JJ's Dance Club	1850.00	
140	A.R.--Funky Club	1640.00	
150	Supplies--Office	110.00	
160	Supplies--Music & Equip	832.00	
170	Prepaid Insurance	300.00	
220	A.P.--Electronics Unlim.		67.00
230	A.P.--R&B Music, Inc.		145.00
310	Rico Sanchez, Capital		2500.00
320	Rico Sanchez, Drawing	670.00	
410	Service Sales		9050.00
510	Advertising Expense	310.00	
530	Miscellaneous Expense	240.00	
560	Rental Expense	1190.00	
570	Repair & Cleaning Expense	242.00	
580	Utilities Expense	158.00	
	Totals	11762.00	11762.00

SEPTEMBER 26-30

Step 1 Bring up the *Automated Accounting* system.

Step 2 Select data file SANCHEZ XXX XXX (where the Xs are your first and last name) from the drive and directory/folder that contains your data files.

Step 3 Refer to the Problem Instructions.

Step 4 Key the transactions dated September 26-30, and perform the Bank Reconciliation activity.

Hand in the audit report for September 26-30 and any printouts to your instructor.

September 26

No. 51. Paid cash for insurance on van, $360.00. C25.
No. 52. Sold DJ services to a private party; received cash, $345.00. R14.

September 27

No. 53. Paid cash for office supplies, $105.00. C26.
No. 54. Sold karaoke services to a private party; received cash, $300.00. R15.

September 28

Bank Reconciliation. On September 28, Rico Sanchez, Disc Jockey received a bank statement dated September 26. The following information is obtained from the bank statement and from the records of the business. Prepare a bank statement reconciliation. Click the "Other" tool bar button and reconcile the bank statement.

Bank statement balance as of September 26	$4,453.00
Outstanding deposits:	
September 26	345.00
September 27	300.00
Outstanding checks:	
Nos. 21, 23, 24, 25, and 26	
Bank service charge	15.00
Checkbook balance on Check Stub No. 27	$4,250.00

No. 55. Received bank statement showing September bank service charge, $15.00. M6.

No. 56. Sold DJ services to the local country club; received cash, $400.00. R16.

September 29

No. 57. Sold karaoke services to a private party; received cash, $300.00. R17.

September 30

No. 58. Replenished the petty cash fund, $45.00: miscellaneous expense, $30.00; office supplies, $15.00. C27.

No. 59. Paid cash to owner for personal use, $250.00. C28.

No. 60. Sold DJ services to a private party; received cash, $325.00. R18.

Compare your trial balance with the trial balance shown in Figure 3. Find and correct any errors before proceeding.

SEPTEMBER 30—END-OF-FISCAL-PERIOD WORK

Step 1 Bring up the *Automated Accounting* system.

Step 2 Select data file SANCHEZ XXX XXX (where Xs are your first and last names) from the drive and directory/folder that contains your data files.

Step 3 Refer to the Problem Instructions.

Step 4 Key the transactions dated September 30.

Hand in the audit report for End-of-Fiscal-Period September 30 and any printouts to your instructor. Complete the Think Like an Accountant activity on pages 15 and 16.

Adjustment Information, September 30

Office supplies on hand	$ 45.00
Music & equipment supplies on hand	370.00
Value of prepaid insurance	380.00

Figure 3 Trial Balance, September 30

Rico Sanchez, Disc Jockey
Trial Balance
09/30/--

Acct. Number	Account Title	Debit	Credit
110	Cash	4965.00	
120	Petty Cash	150.00	
130	A.R.--JJ's Dance Club	1850.00	
140	A.R.--Funky Club	1640.00	
150	Supplies--Office	230.00	
160	Supplies--Music & Equip	832.00	
170	Prepaid Insurance	660.00	
220	A.P.--Electronics Unlim.		67.00
230	A.P.--R&B Music, Inc.		145.00
310	Rico Sanchez, Capital		2500.00
320	Rico Sanchez, Drawing	920.00	
410	Service Sales		10720.00
510	Advertising Expense	310.00	
530	Miscellaneous Expense	285.00	
560	Rental Expense	1190.00	
570	Repair & Cleaning Expense	242.00	
580	Utilities Expense	158.00	
	Totals	13432.00	13432.00

Figure 4 Post-Closing Trial Balance, September 30

Rico Sanchez, Disc Jockey
Trial Balance
09/30/--

Acct. Number	Account Title	Debit	Credit
110	Cash	4965.00	
120	Petty Cash	150.00	
130	A.R.--JJ's Dance Club	1850.00	
140	A.R.--Funky Club	1640.00	
150	Supplies--Office	45.00	
160	Supplies--Music & Equip	370.00	
170	Prepaid Insurance	380.00	
220	A.P.--Electronics Unlim.		67.00
230	A.P.--R&B Music, Inc.		145.00
310	Rico Sanchez, Capital		9188.00
	Totals	9400.00	9400.00

Name ______________________________

RICO SANCHEZ, DISC JOCKEY

Audit Report
September 1-14

1 Number of debits made to Cash .... ______________

2. Number of credits made to Cash .... ______________

3. Number of debits made to Miscellaneous Expense .... ______________

4. Total debit or credit balance on trial balance .... ______________

5. Number of accounts on trial balance .... ______________

Name ______________________________

RICO SANCHEZ, DISC JOCKEY

Audit Report
September 15-25

1. Number of debits made to Cash .... ______________

2. Number of credits made to Cash .... ______________

3. Number of debits made to Advertising Expense .... ______________

4. Total debit or credit balance on trial balance .... ______________

5. Number of accounts on trial balance .... ______________

Name ______________________

RICO SANCHEZ, DISC JOCKEY

Audit Report
September 26-30

1. Number of debits made to Cash .... ______________
2. Number of credits made to Cash .... ______________
3. Number of debits made to Rico Sanchez, Drawing .... ______________
4. Total debit or credit balance on trial balance .... ______________
5. Number of accounts on trial balance .... ______________

Name ____________________

RICO SANCHEZ, DISC JOCKEY

Audit Report
End-of-Fiscal Period September 30

1. Total of debits or credits for adjusting entries .... ____________
2. Net income for period .... ____________
3. Component percentage for total operating expenses .... ____________
4. Component percentage for net income .... ____________
5. Number of assets on balance sheet .... ____________
6. Total amount of assets on balance sheet .... ____________
7. Number of liabilities on balance sheet .... ____________
8. Total amount of liabilities on balance sheet .... ____________
9. Total amount of liabilities and owner's equity on balance sheet .... ____________
10. Total debit or credit balance on post-closing trial balance .... ____________

Think Like an Accountant
Financial Analysis Activity

The budget for Rico Sanchez, Disc Jockey, for the month of September, is given below.

Rico Sanchez, Disc Jockey			
Budget			
For the Month Ended September 30, 20–			
			% of Sales
Revenue:			
Service Sales		10,300.00	
Expenses:			
Advertising Expense	20.00		
Insurance Expense	260.00		
Miscellaneous Expense	250.00		
Office Supplies Expense	165.00		
Music & Equipment Supplies Expense	450.00		
Rental Expense	1,100.00		
Repair & Cleaning Expense	230.00		
Utilities Expense	155.00		
Total Expenses		2,630.00	
Net Income		7,670.00	

Instructions:

a. Calculate and record the component percentages for sales, total expenses, and net income for the September budget. Round percentage calculations to the nearest 0.1%.

b. After reviewing the budget, Mr. Sanchez decided to increase his advertising budget in the hopes of increasing revenue and net income. Analyze the budget and actual September income statement. Did Mr. Sanchez meet his goal of increasing revenue and net income in terms of dollar amounts? Comment on the change in component percentages for Total Expenses and Net Income from budget to actual.

c. Would you recommend that Mr. Sanchez continue this strategy? Why or why not?